As I Walk Through Life

As I Walk Through Life

A FAMILY'S STRUGGLE FROM THE AZOREAN ISLANDS TO AFRICA

LINA DAPONTE

authorHOUSE®

AuthorHouse™
1663 Liberty Drive
Bloomington, IN 47403
www.authorhouse.com
Phone: 1-800-839-8640

© *2011 by Lina DaPonte. All rights reserved.*

No part of this book may be reproduced, stored in a retrieval system, or transmitted by any means without the written permission of the author.

First published by AuthorHouse   10/17/2011

ISBN: 978-1-4670-6197-1 (sc)
ISBN: 9781-4670-6199-5 (ebk)

Library of Congress Control Number: 2011918326

Printed in the United States of America

Any people depicted in stock imagery provided by Thinkstock are models, and such images are being used for illustrative purposes only.
Certain stock imagery © Thinkstock.

This book is printed on acid-free paper.

Because of the dynamic nature of the Internet, any web addresses or links contained in this book may have changed since publication and may no longer be valid. The views expressed in this work are solely those of the author and do not necessarily reflect the views of the publisher, and the publisher hereby disclaims any responsibility for them.

CHAPTER 1

LIFE ON THE ISLAND

The sun is peeking through the small window, but I am too lazy to get out of bed. I can hear the birds flying outside. Even the rooster is telling me it is time to get up, but it feels like I just went to bed one hour ago; does this rooster ever sleep?

I can smell Mommy's coffee. She must have gotten up very early, and she always gets up early to make breakfast before Dad leaves for work at the American air base. The smell of freshly brewed coffee sweetened with condensed milk is a morning tradition, or it is just a heavenly way to get out of bed. It's Ricory, and the aroma fills the house like a sweet morning smell of the flowers after a rainy day. With bread and homemade butter, it's a breakfast made for a king.

The sea breeze is in the air, breathing softly against my window. I can hear the sea gulls cry and the waves beating against the rocks behind the house, but I am too lazy still. I hear Mom calling, "It's time to get up, or you will waste a beautiful morning lying in bed." It's just like Mom to make us feel guilty. Yes, the sun is up, but that does not mean I have to get up too.

But the smell of the coffee seems irresistible, and I don't want to let Dad leave for work before he gives us the morning blessing. By tradition in the islands children have to ask the mother and father for blessing every morning, after work, and before going to bed, and there are no exceptions.

Dad is sitting at the table with the cups in front of him when I come out of my room, still rubbing my eyes. "Good morning, Dad, Mom. Please bless me."

"God bless you," I hear him say as he pours the hot coffee into a cup and slides it over to me. Life is good, or so I think. Another voice behind me asks for their blessing, and one by one we drink the warm cup of coffee and turn around and go back to bed. Mom and Dad, sitting at the table, whisper softly so as not to disturb the ten sleepyheads who want to sleep just a little more.

Life in the Azorean Islands, as I remember it, was quiet and simple. Dad managed to take care of the land and work at the American airbase as a mechanical engineer. We had a lot of vineyards and fruit trees; we were one of the few families that lived well on the island. The vineyards surrounded the house down the hill a couple

As I Walk Through Life

of miles to the stone wall by the road; they continued on the other side of the road that went across the property. Harvest time was a community affair; each family took a turn harvesting the grapes and making the wine, and even the women and children helped.

Mom did not work on the land unless it was a season like harvest time when every person counted and was needed. She took care of the home and the children (there were plenty of us to keep her busy). She did a lot of sewing for us as well as for income. Since we lived mostly off the land, we also had some chickens and pigs for home consumption, and they were Mom's responsibility.

Around the property there was a very high stone wall that seemed to have been there forever; on the inside of the wall there was a step that allowed us to safely watch the bullfights on the street, one of the island traditions that they still have today. Once a year they run the bulls through the streets, and only the young men and the young at heart would dare tease the bull and get away without being caught.

The large metal gate had a huge medallion that represented the coat of arms of the family that decades before had built and owned that part of the island. We also had a coat of arms from my mother's side of the family, but this is a part of my ancestry that I know very little about. She used to tell us that we had blue blood, a comment that did not make much sense when we were small and cost me a lot of laughs and teasing from the other children when I was in grade school. To my surprise, one day when I cut myself, there was no blue blood. I could not understand why Mom would tell us we had blue blood.

3

At that time I didn't understand the meaning of it, but I knew it had to do with my great-great-grandfather, who used to be very important in the islands and was related to a royal family line. Mom used to tell us stories about this distinguished man who used to ride on a horse through the streets of St. Sebastian, the area where she was born.

As I Walk Through Life

We were a happy family. I am sure that Mom and Dad worked very hard to provide for so many children, or so it seemed. I don't remember my parents going through hard times. We had everything we needed, and Mom and Dad seemed to be happy with us and each other.

I don't think we were rich in the islands, but life treated us well. My parents made sure we went to school and celebrated all the traditions and holidays. Dad loved to tell us stories after dinner until some of us dozed off to sleep and had to be carried to bed by an older brother or sister. We ran around the vineyards without care and always looked forward to being together for dinner and whatever entertainment Mom and Dad provided before bedtime. Storytelling was very important back then, and it was the only means of family entertainment after all chores were done.

That is how we spent the first years of our lives and where we left our roots and hearts; most of us never returned. For some the memories have become a dream of another life or maybe even a past life, since the memories are so old, and it seems that it was centuries ago. Mom and Dad dreamed, all the rest of their hard lives, of going back home someday. They told us stories of their lives and youth as if they wanted to make sure every detail would be passed on to future generations, and just maybe some of us would finally go home to that simple life.

Chapter 2

SAILING TO THE PROMISED LAND

Our journey to this new life that my mom and dad dreamed of was supposed to be the beginning of a prosperous life with unforgettable experiences. Dad always had a sense of adventure, which I believe was his weakness. He always thought there was more to life than to live on a little island, grow grapes, and raise children. He thought we could have much more than we had.

Portugal was sponsoring families to go to Africa and work the land. They provided a house and all the necessities for the family to start, including all the expenses of the move. They needed people to colonize an unpopulated part of Africa where they would grow wheat that would then be sent to the mainland. I don't know the details of the contract, but most of the crops were given to the Portuguese government. The families would keep part of the profits in exchange for their labor.

I am sure that at some point in his life after leaving the islands, Dad realized that he had made a mistake. But by then it was too late to turn back, and he paid a very high price for that mistake.

I was four or five the day we left the island. Every one of us had this sad feeling of loss, especially mom; she was leaving behind her elderly mother and all her brothers and sisters, every person that she had known all her life, and she knew that she might never see them again.

I remember the big ship, *Niassa*. It seemed big back then, but it was about six hundred feet long, according to my older brothers. Long lines of people were impatient to board it; they could not wait to get to the promised land. For the children this was an adventure, so there were lots of smiles on little faces. However, the adults seemed anxious and unsure; at least that is what I remember seeing on my mom's face. Everyone was sad and tearful: the family staying behind and the ones leaving, especially my grandmother, who knew she was seeing us for the last time. The goodbyes back then were very painful—even the children felt it. Mom, holding my little brother in her arms only a few months old, kept looking back to make sure she would remember the faces that she so much loved fading at a distance at the sound of the enormous ship cutting through the waves. Crossing the immense ocean, the ship was taking us to a new life that was supposed to bring us joy and happiness.

Lina DaPonte

That was what we had always had with our simple life on the island, if only we had known that we didn't have to look any further than our very own backyard.

The trip lasted a little more than thirty days, but it seemed forever. People were sick and tired, and some even died during the journey. I don't remember the quality of the food, but I do remember a huge dining room with many rows of tables. This was not a luxurious ship; the government used it mostly to transport soldiers from Portugal to Africa.

The kids were allowed to play on the deck, and since kids will always be kids, we always had something to do or discover, which made the time go by a little faster. On the other hand, the adults were showing signs of impatience from being confined to a limited space and having to share that space with strangers from all walks of life. There were a lot of tears and trepidation even before the ship arrived at our destination. I guess after a while people need space to survive, or some will become like animals in a cage.

Mom tried to keep us always together, especially because people were getting sick with measles, mumps, chicken pox, and other diseases that could not be contained properly in such a small space, posing the danger of an epidemic on the ship. I know that some of us had the measles and spent most of the voyage in the ship's infirmary or confined to the cabins for the greater part of the trip.

Just before Cape Hope in South Africa, the seas were very rough, and the ship was taking some water. We were rescued—or helped, I should say—by a South African ship and spent a few days docked on Cape Hope for repairs. We were not allowed to leave the ship because of the endemic illnesses. We left a few days later, on our way to the southeastern coast of Africa.

After we arrived at Lourenço Marques (now called Maputo), a port on the Indian Ocean in Mozambique, we were taken in buses to a rice and wheat plantation, where we had a house and food prepared by the neighbors for the new arrivals. I remember when we arrived at the colony, tired and hungry, the neighbors had made bread and some food. I don't remember what it was, but we were so tired that anything tasted good.

The next morning there was a lot of commotion and people stopping by, some just out of curiosity and some to make sure we were okay and had all our basic needs met. The women took Mom to see the big brick oven where they baked the bread; I guess each family took turns with its use. The laundry was also done in a big tank shared by all the women in the colony. By this time Mom was starting to realize the kind of life we had gotten ourselves into.

Lina DaPonte

Mom was very shy and humble, and her children were always properly behaved and properly dressed. This did not match the population and the culture where we had landed. The children walked barefoot, and their clothes were rough and in need of washing. Our neighbors were teasing us about our little pretty dresses, which would soon change: like the other children we had to help with the crops and with the harvest. That was the cruel reality which Mom and Dad had not planned on; they wanted us to go to school, but child labor was a way of life in the colony. That was one reason they preferred large families.

In the Portuguese colony, we were provided with everything we needed for survival, but we did not own our lives or decide what to do. We needed permission from an established group in charge of any issues between the people and the government. We were not allowed to leave the colony and move to another part of the country without the risk of imprisonment. When I think back, I don't see much difference between this life and slavery or communism; it definitely wasn't a democracy. I don't think Mom and Dad were ready for this kind of life, and this was not the life they had in mind for us.

School was limited to elementary level, and even at that level it was based on the need to be able to read and write. Parents were not obligated to send a child to school if the child was needed to help with the land. One situation in particular seemed to awaken my dad to the reality of the situation.

I remember going with my parents and my brothers and sisters to the wheat plantation. We had a barn for the cows, since the means of transportation was either cows or horses pulling a wagon. Some people after a while would save enough to by a tractor, but that took some time, and we were just starting.

As I Walk Through Life

My older brothers would help Mom and Dad work on the rice and wheat, and the younger ones would watch the cows or other animals that we had on the farm. I remember Dad asking me to go to the barn and let one of the bulls out to eat; he was going to use this bull to pull the wagon to go back home. I went inside the barn, and all I could see was this huge animal that scared me to my bones. I hid in a corner of the barn until Dad came and looked for me.

When I think back today, I imagine the danger that we had to face and my parents' need to put us in that situation to survive in that environment and culture. It was then that dad realized the serious mistake and the misleading information by the Portuguese government to these families. It was not about giving us a better life; it was about colonization and growing crops to send back to the mainland as they called it. They had no intentions of providing the children with an education; that was not the main purpose of the colony. They wanted the colony to grow and the people to stay there, and the longer they kept the young people uneducated, the easier it was to keep them in the plantation. Most parents would send their children for basic learning and then take them out of school, since there was no law that children needed to stay in school up to a certain age, and the need for child labor was very high.

A few months after we arrived at the plantation, Mom and Dad decided that this was not what they had bargained for. They wanted us to be able to attend school and get a real education, but they were faced with a lot of resistance and even threats from the colony commissioner if they tried to live without permission. Dad had a contract to work and pay back to the commissioner all the expenses of the move from the Azorean Islands to Africa, otherwise, if he left Africa, he would have to compensate the commissioner

11

Lina DaPonte

for all the expenses, so he would have to find a way to pay for the family to return, and he did not have the means to do it. I am sure that he felt trapped with his family with no option but to accept that way of life. We stayed at the plantation a little over a year, time for Dad to save a little money and buy a wagon so we could plan our escape.

One night, in the wee hours of the morning (so the neighbors would not know Mom and Dad packed the wagon), the family, with a limited amount of food and at God's will, left the colony in the direction of the nearest town, which Dad had visited when he bought the tractor.

We didn't have a home or a place to go, but Dad wanted to get us to the nearest town and then decide what to do next. Mom and Dad were in their forties and had ten children ranging from three or four months to twenty years old. Dad just wanted to get as far as he could from the colony, and with very limited resources, they put their trust and their lives in the hands of God and followed the only dirt road that Dad was familiar with to take us somewhere away from the colony and give us a chance to start over.

CHAPTER 3

ESCAPE TO THE SUGARCANE
PLANTATION

I still remember the adventurous journey, Mom sitting inside the wagon and breastfeeding my young sister. At least she had a decent meal; we did have plenty of bread and cheese, so we did not starve. But that wasn't the only thing they had to worry about. The unfamiliar land full of dangerous wildlife and so many children for them to care for did not make the trip easy for them or us.

Some of the youngest took it as an adventure without minding the danger and the difficult situation that the family was in. I remember Mom telling us to close our eyes and try to sleep, and soon all would be over, and we would be home safe. It was dark, hot, and humid. I could hear sounds coming from all around us. I never knew that the night had so many sounds. The trees seemed to be taller than normal; in fact, at night I could not tell where the trees ended. They were so tall that they looked like they were touching the dark blue sky full of little stars, and the unpaved road didn't seem to go anywhere.

There was no human life around; once in a while I could hear a faint sound of drums and a humming song coming from some distant native village in the middle of

13

Lina DaPonte

the jungle. It was a long night. I remember sleeping on and off, but the humps and the bumps were so hard that only exhaustion would allow sleep to take over.

I don't know how far we were from the colony when the sun finally came out and Dad finally stopped for a stretch and to pick some fruits that were abundant in that part of the country. He also needed the rest, since he'd been awake all night trying to gain time and distance. He took a little nap under the shade of a masala tree, and we had a chance to play and be kids for a little while. But the sun was too hot, and after a short rest we had to get back on the road to reach the next village before nightfall.

It was late in the afternoon when we finally arrived at the Village of Marracuene. Dad stopped somewhere on the center of the village across from a cantina. He told us not to leave the wagon and wait for him to come back; he needed to ask for directions and help from the people there. It was very obvious for the people of the village that we were in serious need of help.

Soon after Dad went inside the cantina, some people came out to greet us and bring us some food. They looked very friendly and willing to help. It was good to see some friendly faces, but we were scared and tired; we just wanted to go home. Mom kept trying to smile and reassure us that everything was going to be okay, but I could see in her eyes that she was hiding fear and pain. She felt out of place and very fragile with a little child on her arms and another nine, some of them not much older. I could hear her murmur a little prayer for help. If we had to continue to the next village, it would be another day and night on the wagon not knowing where we were going.

As I Walk Through Life

After a while Dad came out of the restaurant with a smile on his face. *This must be our lucky day,* I thought, but why would Dad be smiling when we were so tired, with no place to go? *Why doesn't Dad take us to the ship so we can go back home where we belong?*

But God had something else for us: a rich family was looking for a family willing to live and work on their sugarcane plantation not far from the village on a nearby island of Macaneta. The person in charge of the plantation at the time was looking for a replacement family, and we appeared just at the right time—or maybe God was giving us the help we desperately needed.

Since the island was thinly populated, except for some native villages, which made a living from the plantation and from fishing, it was hard to find someone willing to live there. So for us it was our lucky day and a gift from heaven, and Dad's decision was obvious. We were desperate, and this offer was perfect. Life was good, and luck was on our side.

One of the men told Dad to follow his tractor, and he was going to take us there. Apparently he had the responsibility of taking care of the plantation until they found someone more permanent. Mom was a little confused, but I could see some hope in her eyes. I remember Dad telling her that we had found a home to live in; we were going to a sugarcane plantation just on the other side of the river, on a small island called Macaneta. We could live there, and the children could go to school in the village. He also told Mom that we were only a couple of hours from the capital, which offered other possibilities for my three older brothers and sister. They were still young but were beginning to look toward a life of their own, and the city was a good place to start.

Lina DaPonte

We had to cross a river on an old wooden ferry pulled by ropes attached to each side of the river. It appeared to be about four hundred feet wide at that point, the current was strong, and hippos and crocs were abundant in that part of the island. The ferry was an enormous wooden platform that carried everything, including the tractor and wagon, across the river. On either end of the ferry about ten men stood pulling the ropes that moved the platform back and forth all day long. It was the only means to get to the island, since there was no bridge to go across—one reason the island had very little population.

The experience of the ship crossing was nowhere close to the experience of crossing this river. As the men pulled the rope in unison, they sang a song that would give them the energy and the rhythm to pull the next stroke, I could not understand what they were singing but I remember thinking, *This is beautiful, and we're going to have a place to live for the first time since we left the colony*. Everybody seemed happy. Mom was smiling with excitement; she was beautiful, but she was even more beautiful when she was smiling with happiness. Dad looked like a kid at Christmas time. He was moving around, making sure we all got in the ferry and everything was all right.

The sun was like burning flames in the sky. The men pulling the ferry, half-naked, were sweating so much that I didn't know if it was from the heat or from the splashing of the river. Their voices tuned to each stroke as they pulled the rope. The sound of the water against the ferry was somehow magical; only Africa can give you that feeling. I was in love with everything, the sounds, the magic, and the people. Somehow I felt at home.

As we stopped on the other side of the river, there were a lot of native children playing and singing. They

As I Walk Through Life

did not see white people that often, especially a bunch of white kids fully clothed. To us, the native kids looked kind of funny. They wore very little clothing, and some had no clothes at all except strings of colorful beads around their necks and ankles. If they looked curious about us, we were even worse. They were nice and friendly, touching our hair and smiling; since we could not understand each other, that was all we could do to communicate, but it didn't take long for us to start playing with them.

We were welcomed at the plantation by a group of native workers and their families. These were the people who would take care of us and with whom we would live our daily lives. They became our extended family for the next twelve months on the sugarcane plantation.

Wandering around the plantation, I smelled roasted corn and peanuts. The native women would sit on the floor in front of a little fire and roast corn. There were a lot of curious eyes on us; the children were touching us like we were not real, or so it seemed to me at the time. To my surprise, I was not scared; in fact I was so in love with everything that it didn't seem real.

The plantation was a beautiful house in the middle of nowhere; there were miles and miles of sugarcane around the house and the ocean not too far beyond. As I heard the sound of the waves crashing against the sand and felt the breeze off the water and the warmth of the sun in my heart, a vision of home now so far away went through my mind. There was a resemblance, not exactly the same but close enough for us to feel at home again. Our excitement was so great that the fatigue from the journey was now gone.

We ran inside the house. It was just like a palace. We had a beautiful home back in the Portuguese Azores,

Lina DaPonte

but this one was the biggest house I had ever seen. The furniture was very fancy and different from what we had back home. I remember thinking that the people who owned it must have been very rich. Mom and Dad looked like kids going from room to room with peaceful but excited smiles on their faces.

Everything was so perfect that at first it felt like a dream, but if it was, I didn't want to wake up. After this wonderful burst of energy, running in and out of the house, trying to see everything and keep this moment as long as I could. Mom put us to bed. I was very tired and sleepy. The sounds of the night at the sugarcane plantation were different from the islands with the exception of the ocean. I heard the sound of distant drums and the natives of the island singing monotonous songs to the beat of the drums. I remember thinking they must be celebrating our arrival; why else would they be singing this late at night? It was with this wonderful sound that I drifted to sleep until the next day.

CHAPTER 4

LIFE AT THE PLANTATION

Waking up at the plantation was very strange. For the first few minutes I didn't remember were I was, but it was comfortable and warm. I didn't smell Mom's coffee like I used to back home, but I did smell food, and since our last meal was not much to brag about, I was ready to eat anything Mom prepared. I listened in silence for the old rooster, but there were too many new sounds that I didn't recognize. I could hear the ocean and people talking outside. I could hear Dad talking to somebody but could not recognize the voices or what they were saying.

It was very warm, and the sun was peeking through the windows. I finally heard Mom and some of my brothers and sisters. I started to remember the events of the night before and our arrival at the plantation and the big house. I was not dreaming after all; it was time to get up and see what was happening. I had much to see and much to explore in this beautiful place that we landed up in.

I peeked through the kitchen door and saw a few natives with baskets of vegetables and fruits I didn't recognize that looked very good. They even had fresh goat milk. I had never had goat milk, but it tasted good. That morning, we had hot cereal made from corn flour and flat bread made on top of the woodstove that smelled

19

Lina DaPonte

like the roasted corn I had smelled the day before. There was also a bowl of fresh honey and brown sugar from the plantation. We could eat all we wanted; there was plenty more. Dad ate eggs fresh from the chicken coop, and there was coffee. Although it didn't smell like what we used to have in the islands, it smelled very good too.

After breakfast Dad met with the workers of the plantation. He needed to go to work and learn about his new responsibilities. and he had a lot to learn. The people were more than willing to teach him and show him around. I went outside to check things around the house. I could hear some children laughing, and I wanted to see them again.

My brothers and sisters and I soon made friends with the native children and began to explore the area and our new home. The house stood on top of a hill just like our house on the island, but it was much bigger and built on a different design. There were lots of trees around the house full of fruits that I didn't recognize or remember eating. The sugarcane began down the hill next to a small stream of fresh water, and we could see miles of it. There were a lot of pineapples and coconut trees, and of course what would become my favorite fruits the mango and *cajú*, the fruit of the cashew tree.

There were also lots of colorful birds and even little monkeys jumping from branch to branch and making loud noises. I had never seen monkeys except in the little zoo we had back home. They didn't seem upset by our presence, but I think they were also curious to see new people around. There were a lot of chickens and goats just mingling around. The animals didn't seem to be worried about the people, and nobody bothered them. This struck me because back in the islands and at the colony, all

20

As I Walk Through Life

the animals were confined to certain areas; here at the plantation they were free to walk around without care.

Around the property there were some little houses for the native families that cared for the property, helped with the house chores or minded the yard and the animals. Mom didn't have to do much except take care of us, especially my little sister, who was only several months old. There were always some native women or men following us around to make sure we were safe and did not get into trouble; we were very curious and got into everything. There was always a little fire with food cooking that the natives were happy to offer us, and we were very willing to try it.

After the first few days of unforgettable experiences and learning new things, life started to feel normal, and we could begin to understand the natives and begin to communicate with them. As time passed we began to venture a little further away from the house and visit the native village that was near the ocean that I could hear nearby. The native women were busy pounding the corn to make flour or grinding the peanuts to make milk for cooking. The natives lived mostly on food they grew from the land; there were fishermen who lived from what they caught and sold it to other villages.

Between the native huts and the ocean, a lot of fish covered with salt were spread to dry under the hot sun. This was the way the natives preserved their foods. Some of the sun-dried fish or small shrimp was sold at the nearby village on the markets; this was a way of life for the native people on this small island.

The plantation was the heart of this small friendly island. Most of the population either fished or worked at the plantation. The native women took care of our house

Lina DaPonte

and did the cooking and the cleaning; they also kept an eye on us, a bunch of kids who had no clue of the dangers on the island. We learned to watch out for snakes and other dangerous animals and not to wander through the dangerous woods without an adult. We also learned what fruits to eat and which to avoid.

The children on the island were as amazed with us as we were with them and just as curious. Amazingly, even though we did not speak the same language, we played together and understood each other, and before we knew it, we began communicating in their language or ours. It didn't take long for us to feel at home and familiar with the surroundings. We began to hang out with the native kids like they were part of the family.

Now and then I loved going down to the ocean shore to watch the little fragile canoes cutting through the waves and disappearing under a bright sun. I could hear the crews singing melancholic songs as they threw nets, hoping for a good catch. It was beautiful to hear; they never worked without music and of course they didn't need a radio because they made their very own African songs and music.

At sunset the women would sit on the warm white sand, waiting for the men to come home. The first sign, even before we could see the fragile little canoes on the sunset, was the sight and sound of sea gulls on the wind, announcing their arrival—and of course spreading the news of a possible good meal.

The island did not have electricity, so we used kerosene for lights and a woodstove to cook. Mom learned how to make the best use of the resources available and how the natives preserved the meats, fish, and dried nuts. Dad liked to hunt, so most of the time we had fresh meat or

As I Walk Through Life

fish that fishermen brought us each day. We also grew our own corn, peanuts and different vegetables for our daily consumption. Salt and sugar was abundant in the island; raw and unprocessed though it was, we loved it.

The island was a little paradise on earth. Nobody starved, and there was plenty of food or else the means to grow it. Even our health seemed to be under control with this natural organic living—thank God, because the nearest hospital was on the other side of the river.

There was no medical assistance on the plantation with the exception of a voodoo doctor or the use of natural herbs. I remember one time Dad had to rush my baby sister on the tractor to the ferry and the hospital. My young brother and I were also rushed to the hospital one time due to some poisonous snake; I don't remember exactly how it got to us, but it had to do with Mom killing a turkey that had been beaten.

Soon after we arrived on the island, my older brother and sister, with the help of some people from the village, left for the capital, Lourenço Marques, and stayed there to learn a trade and work. Dad at the time had no means to send them to school to get a better education; he was too busy surviving and taking care of the younger children, so the best option at the time was for them to work or learn a trade since higher education was not then affordable. The rest of us stayed on the island to attend school in the village.

By this time Dad was more or less settled with his responsibilities on the plantation. All he had to do was manage the workers and make sure that the work in the plantation was done. This was not difficult since the natives of the plantation were very friendly and humble. Besides, they were used to this type of life and had been

Lina DaPonte

working with sugarcane forever, since this was their main source of income alongside fishing and cultivating their own crops.

Life was good at the plantation; we could not have been treated with more love or respect from the islanders. It was as if this was their mission and obligation, and it was their honor to serve us freely. My brothers and sisters and I were constantly under watch by the natives, since there was plenty of trouble for us to get into.

Snakes, in particular, were a regular danger. The wild animals weren't much of a threat to children; they would stay clear of the villages and most of the time would attack the small animals, like the chickens and goats. The most aggressive and daring, however, were the snakes, and as expected we did have some casualties among the children. Most times the natives knew how to deal with a snakebite if it was caught within a certain time. Otherwise survival was very rare, since the nearest hospital was in the next village, and we had to cross the river by ferry.

Until Dad arranged for transportation and someone to take us to the village every day and make sure we were safe, he let us attend school with the natives of the island. It was a very basic learning, mainly how to speak the language, basic reading and writing, and a lot of fun. The school, or what was supposed to be a school, was under a huge masala tree just outside one of the native villages, and a missionary was our teacher. It was a fun school, the best I've ever attended. It was a small cabana with four posts and a roof of dry grass and bamboo. The native kids had cleaned the floor with a tree branch or a palm leaf. The only furniture was a small desk and bench of rough-cut wood for the teacher; two small boxes and two small rocks were desks for my sister and me; the

As I Walk Through Life

rest of the children sat either on the floor or on small mats made of grass. Every day the children would pick wildflowers or fruits and place them on top of the little boxes as a welcome to their little school. They had never gone to school with white kids, so having us was an honor to them.

We had no books or pens to write so we each carried a small blackboard with a white charcoal stone as a pen. The best part of it was that we had no homework. We learned how to sing and play new games, we learned how to speak the native language and they learned ours; but of course, since nothing is perfect, we were more interested in the communicating part of the learning. Mom and dad were not very pleased with our educational progress on the island, so they finally arranged for us to go to school across the river in the nearby village of Marracuene, where we had first arrived.

Bur there was the issue of us having to cross the river to and from school, and since Dad did not have a car, we had to walk most of the time unless he had time to take us on the tractor to the ferry and then we would walk home on our way back; sometimes we would catch a ride on a native wagon passing through. Needless to say the population on the island got to know us very well, and there was always someone to make sure we would make it home safe.

The first few weeks of school we were doing okay because we always had an escort to make sure we got there and back. As time passed, though, we began to take charge and walk to the ferry by ourselves, so Dad did not have to worry about our safety or take the time from his busy life to drive us to the ferry in the morning. This was the best time in the island that I remember. On our

25

Lina DaPonte

way to the ferry my older sister and I would play with the native kids all the way there. We would climb trees and make toys out of wood and other things that the native children played with. We would stop at one of the villages and mingle with the people and play with the children, so the trip to school without supervision would take us most of the morning. By the time we made it to school, most of the time it was either very late or at the end of class. This went on for some time until the teacher finally got hold of Mom and Dad and told them that we were not making much progress and missing a lot of school time.

This was a serious situation. For a while Dad did take us to the ferry to make sure we crossed the river on time, but as a long-term solution he did not see that he could keep it up, especially during the harvest of the sugarcane. We had to walk with an escort without stopping here and there to rest, and after we crossed the ferry to the next village, it was a long walk still to get to the school. We complained about it all the time or were too tired by the time we got to class. To make things worse, most of the time the class was halfway done or more.

A year had passed since we moved to the island. Soon my parents realized that, although we had all we needed, living in the middle of pure nature, to grow up happy, we still had a serious issue to handle: providing education to a bunch of kids who were school-aged or quickly reaching that age. Mom and Dad soon began to think seriously about a possible move to the village of Marracuene where we all could attend school without traveling long distances.

Chapter 5

THE MOVE ACROSS THE RIVER TO

MARRACUENE

If there is one thing I have learned since my youth, it is not to take life for granted, because life takes a lot of unexpected turns or it gets in the way, and good things don't last.

By this time, Mom and Dad had learned and got to know the area and the village across from the river. He also learned that most families lived either off the land or from construction jobs, and since the village was constantly growing, there was a good opportunity for him to get a job in construction. Then Mom could take charge of the household and, with the help of a native family that lived in the property we had moved to, grow a vegetable garden for our consumption. There were plenty of fruit trees and a pineapple plantation which would make some money for family income until Dad secured a job in the village.

The native people from the village were also very helpful so Mom would not have to worry about the outside chores. Most of these plantations had native families residing in servant quarters on the plantation to help with

Lina DaPonte

the household and the plantation itself. The family living in the main house were either owners or renters, and the native families would stay with them.

Mom spent most of her time taking care of the family and the property with help from the resident natives. She made our clothing for us, and sometimes she would get a client who needed some seamstress work. She grew adept at it, and eventually she would make some money to help support the expenses of the property and the people working there. Primarily, though, she was running the household because Dad would find jobs always too far from home, so she was pretty much on her own most of the time.

Dad continued to take care of the sugarcane plantation until a new family moved in. Since it did not need constant care—it took a long time to grow, and water was abundant on the island—he had plenty of time to look for another job in the village. He eventually found a job as a carpenter near our new house.

With this move came a change in our peaceful life once more, only this time we didn't have to leave in a rush or in the middle of the night with no place to go to. We still missed our little paradise in the island, but the move to the village was necessary in order to be close to the schools.

The youngest of my three older brothers was in his teens, and the plantation did not have much to offer him. Like the other two, more or less set with jobs in the capital, he was curious about life in the city, so he went to meet them there. This left Mom and Dad with very young children who would now be able to attend school and have the possibility of a normal education.

As I Walk Through Life

The rest of us who were school-aged began going to school and enjoyed making new friends. Mom continued to care for the household and our well-being. One of the native couples that worked at the sugarcane plantation walked with us to the village and helped Mom with the inside chores and the smaller children.

In the meantime Dad began to enjoy his life in the small village and socializing with the other men at the cantina. Since there wasn't much to do in the village, they would play cards and drink, both after work and on his days off. Since everything has its price, Dad began enjoying his drinking and began spending the money that Mom needed to feed her seven remaining kids at home and run a household.

This time we could not survive just from the land, the way we had on the sugarcane plantation. We did have fruits and vegetables and maybe some chickens and rabbits, but most of our food cost money, which she didn't have. With Dad behaving as he was, the money became very scarce and life very difficult. This was no longer living; it was survival.

There is a Portuguese saying, "In the house where there is no bread, there is no peace." Mom and Dad began having some serious arguments about money and Dad's drinking. She was unable to care for seven kids on her own, and Dad was in serious trouble with the excessive drinking; she needed to do something about it. It was the first time I remember Mom and Dad engaging in heated discussions about things not working out and the need to make a serious change.

I don't remember how long we stayed in the village of Marracuene, but I believe it must have been a couple of years before Dad decided to take the family and try

29

Lina DaPonte

his chances in the capital, Lourenço Marques, where my three older brothers were already working and could help us too. So again Mom and Dad packed the few things we had, and with a bundle of kids we hopped on a train and left for the capital.

CHAPTER 6

MOVING AROUND A BIT, FROM SUBURBS TO THE COUNTRYSIDE

This next transition is a little unclear to me, but we landed in the suburbs of the city, and Dad continued to struggle for a good-paying job. He kept pursuing a trade in carpentry, which gave him a better opportunity for jobs. Still, his jobs paid so little that we hardly survived.

By this time my older brother enlisted in the military and was deployed to the north of Mozambique to fight in the civil war between Portugal and the natives of the land. My older sister secured a job in one of the hair salons to learn the trade, so her pay was very little and could not help us that much. Mom had to take care of us, and we were so many that she had little time left to be able to earn a living to help Dad. She did, however, work at home doing some sewing for the neighborhood and making uniforms for the local schools.

We lived in a very poor neighborhood. The houses were made of wood and sheets of zinc. It's a good thing we did not have cold weather in that part of Africa, or we would have been in serious trouble—although I cannot imagine being in any more trouble than we already were.

Lina DaPonte

The neighborhood was mostly Hindu or Muslim Indians. I rather liked this neighborhood; the people dressed differently, their food was different, and even their praying habits was new to me, but we found a way to enjoy and make new friends. In our area everybody struggled to survive, so in that way we were no different. I remember the Muslim people going to the mosque to pray. They used to take off their shoes at the entrance, and I don't remember seeing so many shoes at one time and could not understand how they would know which ones belonged to whom.

Mom used to tell us that the devil runs away from children, and she was right. We were always looking to find some entertainment, so that meant getting in trouble most of the time. I recall one fun time when several other kids and I got in trouble. We went to the mosque, stole all the shoes, and hid them in the woods. Then we waited in hiding to see the people coming out of the mosque and looking for their shoes. Eventually we were caught, returned the shoes, and had a well-deserved punishment—but we did it again a few weeks later.

Mom and Dad continued their struggle. Dad's drinking was not any better; it became a habit and very much part of our lives.

There was a convent nearby (which is where we attended school), and the nuns found out about our family and our struggle for food and other necessities. They used to make a big pot of soup to feed some of the more needy families in the area, and boy, we were definitely in need. I remember carrying this big pot of soup with my sister that smelled like the best meal on earth, so every day we would go there at lunchtime and pick up a huge pot of soup. Even though every day they served almost the

As I Walk Through Life

same soup, over and over again, it tasted as though we were trying it for the first time.

This went on for another couple of years. We were surviving with basic necessities through the help of some good people. The nuns and others made sure we had clothing and shoes and attended school, while Dad was struggling to get a good-paying job to take care of us.

After a couple of years life had not improved much. I was in first grade when Mom and Dad decided to try another move to a farm area outside the city. There we could work the land while Dad went to work. This at least would give them the opportunity to grow some chickens and vegetables, and we would not go without a good meal or have to take charity from other people. Mom wanted us to be able to sustain ourselves with some level of dignity.

She took care of us, and with the help of a native couple that lived on the property, we had lots of vegetables and fruits. This time we had plenty of food resources from the land, and with Dad working, life got a little better. However, there are no roses without thorns; we also had a few we needed to overcome in order to enjoy our new home. The closest school was a mission of priests and nuns far from the area; it took us over one hour to walk

I was about eight years old by this time when we began school at the nearest Catholic mission. A lot of children walked from long distances, so we were not the only ones. Good thing the crime was low at that time and hitching a ride was a very common thing even for school kids to do. There weren't too many schools so walking long distances to school was a normal thing.

Regularly people would stop and offer a ride to a bunch of kids; other times we used to catch the bus that was always full and sit at the back. The bus attendant

33

Lina DaPonte

used to start collecting the tickets or the money from the front; by the time he got close to us, we would ring the bell to get out. (Money was tight so mom and dad could not afford to pay the bus fee for all of us.) Most of the time we would still have some walking to do, but at least we had gained some distance. We did this all the time, and I am sure the bus attendant knew we were hitching a free ride, but he pretended not to notice it. After all, it was a custom to give rides to children going to school.

We moved one more time when I was going to school at the mission, but this time we were only half as far from the school, so we didn't mind so much. With some struggle my parents continued to try to better their lives one day at a time.

CHAPTER 7

ESTABLISHING ROOTS

During our time in the countryside, my oldest sister, now a young (and single) woman, became pregnant. Dad was too old-fashioned to accept her pregnancy and another mouth to feed, so she left home to try to survive in a nearby city. God is always watching, though, and as they say, everything happens for a reason. She got on a bus, crying and catching the attention of the bus driver, a divorced young man with three children to care for on his own. They eventually moved in together and stayed together the rest of their lives.

About a year later—I must have been in second grade at the time—she returned home to make peace. My father was a stubborn man, fixed in his old ways, but it is true that blood is thicker than water. Looking at his new granddaughter softened his heart, and finally they made peace.

This was a great day. I remember it clearly. My sister seemed so happy with her new family, and making peace with Dad allowed her to see the rest of the family that she missed so much.

Maybe another year later Dad decided to move to another area outside the city. Development was going on there, and the government was selling land at very

Lina DaPonte

low cost. His intentions were to be able to get a piece of land to call his own, so we didn't have to move again. He wanted to finally put down some roots, because we were growing up. Both my father and my sister and her husband decided that this was a good place to raise kids. It was a new town with a new school and church, but best of all, we didn't have to walk long distances anymore.

We first moved to a rental property and later on to our brand-new home that Dad built for us. Since we lived near the ocean, Dad even built a boat to go fishing. I always enjoyed the ocean, and Dad and the rest of the family seemed to share the same feeling. We spent a lot of time fishing and swimming on a nearby salt lake. Dad was a good swimmer, and we all learned how to sink or swim with him. I remember a little island that we called the monkey island because a lot of small monkeys lived there. We liked to go there to spend the day clamming, fishing, and swimming with Mother Nature.

Life was hard for a large family but we were growing up with some happiness and a future on the arising. School was close by, and with my sister and her extended family living close by, things seemed normal and sometimes almost perfect.

CHAPTER 8

DAD GOES TO SOUTH AFRICA

A few years later Dad decided to move to South Africa in search of a life better than what we had. There was a lot of demand for carpenters and construction laborers, so Dad decided to try his luck there, while mom stayed behind taking care of the kids. The plan was that Dad soon would be able to take us with him to live there.

Living alone in South Africa did not help Dad's drinking, and by the time he came home, he was a full-fledged alcoholic and a completely different man. The family was no longer his priority except for the few times that he was able to stay sober. He even became abusive toward my mom to a degree we had never seen before. There were some rocky moments during this time and dad stayed away for long periods.

I believe he was there for three or four years, at times without sending money home except when he came to visit. Mom began to work as a seamstress, trying once again to make a living without Dad's help. Things did get worse during this period of our lives, but some of us had little jobs to help Mom and tried to stay in school at night after work. She still had some children in school who were not old enough to hold a little job. Altogether there were still seven of us at home.

Lina DaPonte

It was at this time that Dad had an accident in South Africa and decided to come home to stay, just in time to keep the family together. He continued to drink but not as much anymore and life seemed to go back to normal. We were a family of survivors, and we were still together except for the three oldest, who were taking care of their own lives

Mom and Dad loved the holidays and tried to maintain the traditions from the Portuguese islands. Dad had built a brick oven for her just like the one she had back home. She liked to bake her own bread at Christmas time or holidays, as well as the traditional *alcatra*, a roasted meat that is such a tradition in the Portuguese islands, and of course we must not forget the sweet bread. I could go on and on with my memories of the foods, but I can't even remember them all.

Dad used to pick the biggest tree he could find that resembled a pine tree; these were very rare in hot climates. The decorations were made by hand; Mom had a special talent to come up with the prettiest decorations I have ever seen. Nothing was bought, since money was a scarce commodity, besides; making the decorations ourselves made Christmas a lot more special.

She made sure we all wore new clothes on Christmas Day; that was very important for good luck, even if it was just a pair of socks. Dad used to wake up on Christmas very early and get us out of bed; this was no day to sleep late. We used to have dried figs and walnuts and sweet bread for breakfast. This was a feast and a very special time.

After breakfast Dad would distribute the gifts to all of us, which was usually one gift and most of the time clothes that Mom had made especially for that day. Mom

As I Walk Through Life

played guitar, and we loved to hear her sing songs that she had learned when she was young; she was quite a singer and a dancer too. Although Mom's life raising ten kids after she left the Portuguese islands became a roller coaster of hard times, she was a lady. Even if she wore a rag for a dress, she made it look beautiful on her. She loved to dress up whenever she could, and so did Dad. They were quite a handsome couple, and even though Dad was hard on Mom and us when he drank to excess, they did love each other very much.

Mom was a very attractive woman with the softest blue-gray eyes. She had the most loving personality, and even her three stepkids truly looked at her as a real mother. Till this day my dad's first family and his second family were always one.

I don't remember much about my father's first wife or his side of the family. He hardly ever talked about it. His first wife died during a plague of leprosy that devastated the island of Saint Michael where he was born and lived with her and their three children, the youngest only one to two years old. After his wife died during the plague, he could not take care of his children, so my two older brothers were placed in an orphanage, and the youngest was placed with one member of his late wife's family.

Dad left Saint Michael for Terceira, trying to build a new life so that he could go back and get his children. This was when he met Mom, a young lady born and raised with the best there was, according to my aunt, her older sister who still alive this day. Their great grandfather's house later became a museum in the city of Saint Sebastian on the island of Terceira. According to the story, he was the richest man on the island, but by the time he died, he had

39

Lina DaPonte

lost most of his fortune, and his home was taken by the government as a patrimony of the island's history.

I wish I knew more about my ancestors, but when I was young and Mom used to talk about them, I thought it was just a fairy tale, and of course I didn't want the kids in school to tease me, thinking that I was making up the story. For years I never thought about how rich my family line was. I hope that before I die I will go back to see where my roots started, or maybe my children will.

CHAPTER 9

I GREW UP FAST

For the next few years we were just a normal family with a lot of teenagers getting into trouble and enjoying life. Mom and Dad seemed to be more settled. By this time Dad had cut down on the drinking, even though he enjoyed it occasionally; at least he was more moderate with it. They did love each other very much, or else they would not have overcome so much in their life, still together smiling and doing things together more than ever. Although most of us were grown up, the younger ones still attended boarding school—a very traditional way to keep the young out of trouble and make sure they grew up as good Christians and educated.

Life in Africa was nothing like that in Europe or America. Children, although very naïve and innocent, grew up faster physically than those across the ocean. It was very normal for young women to be married at sixteen and sometimes even younger. I was fourteen years old when I began to grow up really fast.

Dad was building his own boat as I mentioned earlier, when someone stopped to admire the work and ask if he planned to sell it. It was a mature man with a son on his mid-twenties who was going to change the direction of my life forever. If there is any such thing as love at first

41

Lina DaPonte

sight, this was it. It happened to me, and over the next ten years I grew up twenty.

He was my first real love and my hero; he had fought in the civil war in Angola, a Portuguese colony on the west coast of southern Africa. After the war he returned home and began living a very dangerous life that attracted many young people at that time, smuggling diamonds from the Republic of South Africa into Mozambique. It was a quick way to make money and he had chosen that path.

The rumor went around in the neighborhood that he was interested in me. I was fourteen years old at the time and had never been exposed to womanhood or life as we see on television today. I understood little about men, and I had no idea what sex was about but I remember feeling deeply in love the day he laid eyes on me.

The voice of the people travels fast, though, and my dad and older brothers found out the type of life he was living. They didn't want me in the middle or part of it. Besides, I was too young to be exposed to that type of life and didn't know any better.

My older brothers asked Dad to put an end to it. He did try to stop the relationship, along with my older brothers and sisters, but by then my heart was too blind with love—and I was also very pregnant. I moved in with him and his parents. I could not imagine my life without him and did not have any intentions of listening to my parents or brothers. When he found out that I was pregnant, he immediately arranged for me to have an illegal abortion I was then six months through the pregnancy, and it could not be done. I had no clue what it meant, and I did want the baby, but anything he said I would obey. I didn't know any better and was too young to understand. This is when

As I Walk Through Life

my share of pain began, and during the next ten years I became a woman before my time.

I lost the baby at birth. It didn't make sense at the time. I was going to have a baby and was so happy about it that, when I lost it, I could not understand what had gone wrong or why the baby had died. The years went by, and I was still somewhat separated from my family by my relationship with this man. To them he was an outlaw who sooner or later would be caught, and I would definitely be hurt. They were right, although I didn't get it then.

I used to spend most of my time with his mother doing things around the house. I didn't even go to school at that time; my life revolved around him or waiting for him. At this point my parents had given up, and I was staying at his house most of the time. I did get a little job that got me occupied most of my free time, but at the end of each day, it was him who I waited for—until one day he did not come home.

During one of his regular trips to South Africa, there was a border patrol chase, and his car crashed when he was trying to cross the border to Swaziland. He ended up with brain damage that put him in a vegetative state. For one year I waited at his parents' house for him to come back. I didn't know where he was or even that he'd had an accident. Tired of waiting and not knowing, I had moved back home to my parents when I received the news that he was being brought home as a vegetable.

That day I lost my true love and my hero. I lost the man who had taught me everything I knew. I trusted him with my life, and nothing else mattered. He knew that; he took me as a child and molded me into the woman he wanted; in his own way he loved me and always kept me from being harmed due to his business. He always tried to

43

Lina DaPonte

keep me out of it or even tell me whenever he needed to go away in business.

After I went back home to my parents, my father never really asked me questions about it. At the age of fourteen I was old enough to get married—that was the culture—so whatever was happening, it was my responsibility. For the next year I never heard from him, and his parents would not tell me where he was either. They simply asked me to wait, because he would come for me. This was the hardest part: I never had a chance to say good-bye to him, and just the way he appeared in my life, he left, and there was nothing left for me.

I didn't know how to function without him, so instead of crying for him, I tried to end my life for the first time. I took an overdose of Valium Ten that I managed to convince my friend at the pharmacy that I needed to be able to sleep and get over the rough times. Back home there were no controlled substances, but by having a friend in the right place, we could get anything at a pharmacy, so it was very easy to get the Valium. It didn't work; I was rushed to the hospital just in time for the doctors to force me to throw up the pills.

After this incident I was lost and just wanted to go as far away as I could from the place where everybody kept saying, "I told you so." I was nineteen at the time, and I wouldn't be of age until I turned twenty-one, so I could not do anything without Dad's consent. I managed to get emancipated, misleading Dad about what he was signing, so I could leave the country legally without him knowing. (Instead of learning how to read or write, Dad had to work throughout his childhood to help the family, so he never learned to write anything more than his name. Since he could not read, it was easy to trick him.)

As I Walk Through Life

I had a plan. A friend of mine had gone to Australia, so I made arrangements to meet him in Sydney. My friend from Australia helped me with my flight ticket and a place to stay at the YMCA in Sydney, a home for young women without a home. I got my passport and went to the British Embassy and got my visa and flight confirmation.

One of my sisters found out that I was leaving the country and told Dad. They did try to stop me but it was too late. The document was legal, and they could not stop me from leaving the country. The British Embassy would not dispute the legality of the document, so I left for Sydney, Australia, at nineteen years of age, not knowing exactly what I was doing or how I was going to survive—although my friend had told me that I could easily get a job.

I had never been on my own or away from home, and this trip was definitely away from home. But becoming a mother and losing a child at fourteen, I had experienced pain that I never thought was possible, and having an active sexual life at that age with a mature man had definitely made me grow up fast. Going on this trip could not be any worse. Mom and Dad were very nervous about me leaving home and moving so far away. Besides, emotionally I was not very stable at that time; they were afraid I would hurt myself again, and they wouldn't be there to help.

I did assure the family that I was going to be okay. I had friends in Australia, and if I wanted to hurt myself again, there was nothing anybody could do about it. I needed to get away for a while and maybe start a new life far away from that place. I did promise to return after time passed.

45

CHAPTER 10

ON MY OWN IN AUSTRALIA

My trip to Australia was just as adventurous as my life up to that point. Like people say, the apple does not fall too far from the tree; I was following my dad's footsteps by going from place to place in search of a new life and looking for peace of mind and heart.

Just a few days before I left for Australia, I met a gentleman who was on a business trip in Mozambique from Sydney, Australia. When he learned that I was going there, he gave me his address and contacted his wife to make sure she would help me if I had need. This gave me some confidence and alleviated any fear I had of going to a strange country alone.

He also suggested I contact the YMCA place for young women to stay when traveling alone. The YMCA was located across from the Opera House on the opposite side of Sydney Bridge. From my bedroom window I had a beautiful view of the city. The Opera House looked like a big sailboat on the ocean, and the bridge used to light up like a Christmas tree.

The YMCA was for women between eighteen and twenty-five years of age. There were about fifty young women, and we were all in need of a safe place to stay. The house was supervised by senior women with a lot of

As I Walk Through Life

rules about guests and coming home late. Doors were locked at 10 pm, and in order to stay out late, we needed to request a late key and tell them where we were going and with whom. They cooked all the meals and took care of the linen for the beds and showers.

I enjoyed my time there. I felt protected among people who cared. I shared a bedroom with another young woman who became a great friend to talk to away from home. We had a dress code rule at mealtime, and on weekends they even provided some entertainment, like a movie or even a concert on a small scale. Public transportation in Sydney was mostly trains and subways; I also enjoyed the popular water ferry. I made a lot of friends and even had a couple of young men chasing me.

This was a very serene time in my life. I had the opportunity to focus on myself and reinvent this new and strong person that had been lost along the way. I remember the grand opening of the Opera House in 1974 and Queen Elizabeth's attendance. I did not have the honor of seeing her, but from my bedroom window I had the most wonderful view of the celebration. The ocean in front of the Opera House was full of little sailing boats and lights; it was like looking at a Christmas show.

My stay in Australia was not always roses. I missed my family a lot, especially Mom and Dad, and after six months I returned home to Mozambique. My family were still worried that I was alone in a strange country and afraid that I might do something foolish. But when I told them that I was missing them and wanted to come home, they had tears of joy and opened their arms to my return.

Lina DaPonte

Just before I left for Australia, I had met a young man who kept in touch with me and asked me to come home. So when I got home, we began a relationship that progressed for the following couple of months before the civil war started in Mozambique.

CHAPTER 11

CIVIL WAR AND
THE REFUGEE CAMP

During many years Portugal was sending troops to fight the guerrilla war in the north of Mozambique. The people of Mozambique wanted the war to end with independence from the ruling Portuguese. In 1974 the revolution was already in the south, and crime was on the rise. Nobody was safe anymore, and the guerrillas were putting pressure against the Portuguese government and threatening to take over the country. The rumors of negotiations between Portugal and the guerrillas spread, and the white people were no longer safe. The black people wanted the whites out of their country, so they began attacking the city, killing women and children without mercy.

By this point the war was out of control that the Portuguese army could not protect the white people. The only way to survive was to cross the border to the Republic of South Africa that had offered protection and asylum. First, though, we had to make it to the border, and that was the hardest since the vandalism and killing was everywhere, especially in the areas close to the border.

Lina DaPonte

Finally the Portuguese government ordered the military to form convoys and escort the white people to safety and protection of the South African government. After a night of hell the Portuguese army began patrolling the streets and protecting the people who were trying to reach the safety of the military convoy. I have no words to describe the panic, confusion, and fear of the next couple of days; it was like a dream that left me in a daze.

I hoped it was a dream—that somehow I was going to wake up and everything would be has it was—but the sound of guns, the smell of smoke, and the screams in the night meant another reality that no human being likes to experience.

Just the day before I had gone to work as I always did. I had returned from Australia to my family. I had just started to heal from a painful relationship and was beginning a new relationship that seemed to be going in the right direction—when overnight the country went to hell. I woke up to find everybody running around in turmoil, confused to realize that the war was imminent and safety did not seem to be possible. Families were separated and fleeing for safety. Everywhere you could smell houses burning, and the sound of grenades and guns filled the air. Children saw parents being killed; women were being violated in front of their families and then killed or left to die. I did see a lot of that in the movies, though not even on television: we didn't have TV back then

For two days we got together in groups hoping to build enough resistance to survive any terrorist attack, and most people were not armed or even prepared to defend their own. By the second day some of us were separated and unable to communicate. It became obvious that we needed to seek the safety and protection of the

As I Walk Through Life

Portuguese army, but we did not want to leave without members of the family who were unaccounted for. Through the radio the military broadcast the news that a convoy that would be prepared to move people to safety by crossing the boarder to South Africa, but we needed to get to the convoy somehow and find the family members who had gotten separated during the first two days of the rebellion.

The South African government opened the border to receive those seeking refuge, but to get to the border we needed to make it past the rebels. The military arranged a convoy to the military fort nearest to the border; after that, we were on our own. Some people headed off to the border; some of us did not want to leave without our loved ones, so we waited at the military camp for their arrival.

My mom and I stayed behind waiting for Dad, who was being rescued by one of my brothers and a friend at a construction site away from the city. It was worth the wait when they finally showed up unharmed two hours later. By then most of the family had made it to the border; there most of us found each other. Due to the confusion and the rush to safety, some family members were still separated until we were all taken to the refugee camp and finally got together.

I still remember the day we crossed the border through the barbwire fence and the South African army took us to the camp. They were grabbing the children from their mothers' arms and passing them to strangers; so they were separated in the confusion, and for a while parents didn't know if they would see them again. I remember one young couple with a newborn. To cross the fence, she handed her baby to a soldier, expecting to get the baby back on the other side—but the Red Cross had taken the

Lina DaPonte

baby to safety, and the baby was nowhere to be found until we arrived at a refugee camp. It was heartbreaking to see the desperate parents feeling so helpless.

My family was taken to a refugee camp that became home for us and thousands of other people for the next two months. The South African government began recruiting families and giving them homes and jobs while the emigration officials processed their paperwork.

The refugee camp was located on the mountains of Nelspruit. I wish I had a picture of this time in our lives, but what I have is a memory that time itself will not erase, and it is just as clear as it was thirty-seven years ago. The camp was full of humble people who came to help us, but instead they found refugees with painful hearts who were bitter because of what life was doing to them. Some were missing a loved one, and some were just confused and in denial of the tragic events, but we all had one thing in common: we were entering a new chapter of our lives and had no idea how it was going to end.

The camp was set up with big tents and an endless supply of blankets and mattresses. Volunteers were cooking in big pots and pans to make sure we had enough food. They came from everywhere to help us and comfort us. Every time a load of people arrived, we used to cheer with happiness whether it was a friend, a family member, or just a familiar face who had arrived safe. I don't remember how long we stayed at the Nelspruit camp, but for the next few days the buses continued to arrive.

Soon they had to start moving the people to various improvised camps as the number of refugees grew. After a while people became restless. Women argued constantly, and there were even fights, due to the desperate situation and uncertainty. People were confused and restless; they

52

As I Walk Through Life

had no idea what was going to happen next or if they would ever go back home someday. In the meantime the good people of South Africa didn't know what to do with so many refugees or where to put them. Companies began recruiting workers from the camp. It was a long process but necessary in order to make sure everybody had a home, food, and work.

A few months before the outbreak of the revolution in Mozambique, I was working for an English company that recruited employees to send to the mines and construction work in the Republic of South Africa. Dad never stopped thinking about returning to Johannesburg; his dream was to take his family and move there permanently. On the other hand we knew that the war was imminent, and we would need to seek safety.

While working for Freight Services in Mozambique, I secured a working contract for Dad with a construction company called LTA Construction. The contract would be sent to us so we could move in a safe, organized way, but it had not arrived before we had to flee the country. When we arrived at CULINAN camp near Johannesburg, I contacted the company and let them know that we were at the camp. They immediately sent a van to the camp to fetch us.

To this day I will not forget the young man's face when he arrived. Clearly he was expecting to find a small group of people, and there were sixteen of us ready to go with him. Besides our family, there were some close friends whose had left relatives behind, so we were family to them. Joe was the driver's name, and in no time the sixteen-member DaPonte family were squished inside a small van and headed to Johannesburg at God's mercy. We really didn't know where we were going, but we were

53

Lina DaPonte

safe, out of the camp, and together; nothing else mattered at that time.

Before Joe picked us up at the camp, like all good citizens of South Africa, he spoke with his parents to arrange our food and shelter for the next few days until we had a place to stay, since Dad already had a secured job. When we arrived at Joe's parents' little house, they had no words, there were so many of us. The shock only lasted a moment; the neighbors had already started a campaign for blankets and clothing, and even tents were set up in the backyard for the men to sleep in while the women slept in the house on mattresses placed on every bit of floor they could find. It was a shocking sight to see. By the next morning the neighbors were still coming with food, clothing, or whatever they could give us since we didn't even have a fork to eat with. Dad was taken to his new employer to start working as soon as possible; there was no time to waste. The rest of us still needed to get permits to stay in the country or to be able to work.

The people from the neighborhood finally found a place that could accommodate all of us—an old red-brick building that used to be orthodox religious housing. The building had been transformed into small apartments, and most of them were still empty. For the next few days the neighbors took care of us, and piece by piece they arrived with the things we needed to start our lives in South Africa. With the help of these wonderful strangers, we began to shape our lives to a new beginning.

CHAPTER 12

LIFE IN SOUTH AFRICA AND THE UNITED STATES

A few months after we arrived in South Africa and began to settle down, groups of people began to form a plan to go back and recover our country. Some people were happy to start a new life and put the other behind them, but some just wanted to go home and would not accept their fate and loss. Emotions were still running very high, and groups began to form to go home and overpower the government. A lot of killing went on during the next couple of years, mercenaries were recruited to go back and fight for the country, but as time moved on, people began to count their blessings and go on with their lives.

Lina DaPonte

Pappa and Mamma Da Ponte, facing the future with a smile.

tremendous — we were all feeling very low at the time — and I would like to thank the da Silva's from my heart on behalf of my family."

Obviously, the Da Ponte family couldn't stay in the Da Silva's house for very long — it was bursting at the seams — so José took it upon himself to find the family accommodation work and permits to stay in South Africa.

Dateline's first meeting with the Da Ponte family was in their new accommodation in Turffontein — an incredible redbrick block of flats. The weird, unorthodox design includes turrets, balconies, odd tile roofs and numerous staircases that just don't seem to go anywhere.

No sooner had we stopped in front of the flats when all the Da Pontes, as if by signal, streamed out of the building from all directions. What a welcome, kisses on both cheeks from the numerous Marias, both hands being shaken simultaneously and shy smiles from the dark-eyed children.

One kitchen table, two hard chairs and an enormous bed furnished the lounge. Shirts hung around the walls. A framed photograph of Mamma and Pappa the only decoration. Eighteen Da Pontes crowded into the room, smiling from ear to ear.

Lina told Dateline that Mamma and Pappa Da Ponte had ten children, but one had not left Lourenço Marques with them.

Newly-married Edeltrudes had remained to be with her young husband. She was in the room however, as she'd made a special trip to bring the family's papers. No mention was made as to how this extremely attractive woman had managed to cross the border. She was already making plans to return dressed in the clothes she arrived in . . . black Donovan cap, boys jeans and sports shirt.

At the time of interview, the family was pretty worried as their first application for permission to remain in the republic had been refused. "If we had to go back to Lourenço Marques we'd all be unemployed," said Lina, "Pappa especially. He was a foreman on a construction project but when the trouble started all work stopped. When the heavy rains come the whole project will go back to what it was at the very beginning."

None of the rest of the family's jobs were still available in Lourenço Marques.

Three days after our interview, we heard that the whole family had been granted a further three-months' residence in South Africa. As José da Silva said, "They'll be fine now, the three months will give the rest of the family time to find work. Pappa is already a member of the LTA family."

As I Walk Through Life

SOME ARE REFUGEES...

Dateline felt that this issue was as good a time as any to introduce a few of our immigrant families to the group at large. We chose three families from different parts of the world who, we feel, differ from each other in virtually every possible aspect. Their only common factor being the fact that they are now all part of the LTA family.

First interview was with the 17-strong Da Ponte family from across-the-border Moçambique, a courageous bunch who left everything behind them as they fled strife-torn Lourenço Marques for the safety of South Africa.

The actual interview itself was long and complicated — as was their story — and the fact that only one of the family spoke English certainly didn't simplify matters.

Uncertainty mirrored in a little girl's face.

It goes something like this ...

Head of the family, Joaquim Da Ponte, had met LTA Construction's recruitment officer, José da Silva in Lourenço Marques some time ago. Joaquim, a carpenter, felt that a move to South Africa could be to his advantage and, after an interview, secured a verbal job-offer from José. At this stage, their proposed emmigration to South Africa was to be a planned and orderly operation ... so they thought.

That was before the political power-change in Portugal and the subsequent upheaval in the Portuguese colonies of Angola and Moçambique. 'Pappa' Da Ponte — as he is fondly referred to by his family — realised that strife was eminent. He acted immediately, as his English-speaking daughter Lina described:

"Pappa called the family together and told us we were leaving for South Africa 'chop-chop'. We didn't even have time to pack any possessions or papers. Squeezing our 17-member family into two cars we managed to make it to the border and cross over to the South African side. Our cars had to be abandoned on the Moçambique side so we made our way to the Nelspruit refugee camp by bus."

From the hastily erected refugee camp, Lina contacted José, told him about their position and that her father was anxious to start work with LTA as soon as possible.

Ironically, Joaquim Da Ponte's letter of contract was in the post at the time, so José's instructions were for the carpenter to move to the Cullinan refugee camp, far nearer Johannesburg

José, being a helpful sort of bloke, then asked his parents if they would be prepared to put-up the refugee until suitable accommodation could be arranged. This they readily agreed to.

José had no idea what was in store for him as he set out for Cullinan in the LTA Combi. In his words: "I went to fetch one bloke and found 17 people waiting to go to Johannesburg with me.

"My folks nearly fainted when I arrived at their house with the bulging Combi. We just didn't know where we were going to put them all".

Although shaken, the Da Silva's got to work immediately, racing around the neighbourhood borrowing sleepingbags, tents, groundsheets and bedding from all and sundry. Women and children slept in the house while the menfolk camped outdoors.

"It was pretty choatic," Lina told Dateline, "but far better than the refugee camps. Our first taste of South African hospitality was

The Da Ponte family in their new accommodation.

38

I was among those who would not give up, so I joined a group that was attempting to cross the border to Mozambique and attempt to reclaim our home. I was angry at the world for taking my home, and if we were going to get it back, I wanted to be part of the process. I did make it to the border with a group of other people, including a recruited mercenary. I don't know what our mission was, but the rules were that we would meet

Lina DaPonte

someone at the border, and only at that time they would disclose the plan.

I knew that some people had attempted to cross the border before us and never made it back, but when the emotions are high, it really doesn't matter. We got to the border and our contact never showed up, we knew something had gone wrong so we returned to Johannesburg. It was a long way through the mountains of Nelspruit; we had travelled for fifteen hours, and we were very tired.

The group separated and went different ways. I rode home with the mercenary. After a few hours he decided to stop at one of the many resorts in the mountains. The resort was in the middle of nowhere; people used to go there on hunting trips or travelling across the border to Mozambique before the war.

The resort was very rustic like most resorts in Africa. Because of the political conflict in Mozambique it was nearly deserted, with only a few people. I was tired and just wanted to sleep; my bravery was dying out at that point. I began to wonder what I was doing there, especially with this stranger; after all, he was just a mercenary who had been hired to help the revolutionaries recover the country.

After we had taken a much-needed shower, they prepared us something to eat. Sleepy as I was, I was so hungry that anything would have tasted good. Next to the resort there was a waterfall. We could hear the sound of the water and the wild. The sky in Africa is like no other, and that day it seemed even more beautiful. The revolution was retreating from my thoughts, and a sense of safety and warmth went through my body. I knew then that it

As I Walk Through Life

was time to let go of the war, go home to Johannesburg, and start a new life.

I was blessed to have the opportunity that many didn't. Things happen for a reason, and there are no coincidences. There was a reason in my future that only God knew. I felt humble in the middle of a jungle with the silence of the night and the sounds one hears only in Africa.

We ate in silence, trying to read each other's thoughts. The mercenary's face was tanned from the days spent under the hot sun, but he had no expression; he looked muscular and strong but also beaten down by the life he lived. His eyes were dark like the darkness in the forest around us. I don't know if it was the moment or the flurry of events we had lived the last few hours, but he looked tired, and I just wanted to reach out to him, to his human side.

As if reading my thoughts, he stared at me, probably wondering what I was doing there. We finished dinner and decided to take a little walk. The air was crisp, like most nights in Africa. We'd had some wine at dinner, and I was feeling it. In fact, I don't know if it was the wine, the silence of the night, or loneliness.

He whispered something in my ear that I could not understand—but I could feel his warm breath and the pounding of my heart; my legs felt weak. He put his arms around me and held me there for a long time. His lips were warm and soft, the war was far away, and we were alone in this paradise. Nothing mattered apart from the moment.

We left the resort the next day, never to see each other again. I never regretted that day. It was one of the most beautiful I had, even if it was just one day. We returned home and went on with our lives. Years later I learned

Lina DaPonte

that he had left the war behind and moved to Brazil, but I never heard from him again. It was as the card reader had said to me one day: I was to love and be loved, but I would never be able to keep the man that loved me, and it was a truth that I have experienced over and over again all through my life.

Just as all things in life have an end, so did the hope that we all had to return back home to Mozambique someday. As time went by, the trips to the border also died away, and life began to take a normal path of adjustment. Most of the refugees made South Africa their new home. There were plenty of jobs available for the ones who wanted to settle.

Some returned to Mozambique, hoping to be able to take over where they had left off. Some went to Portugal and joined relatives who had never emigrated. Either way, life was never to be the same again, and no matter where we started a new life, we would always be an emigrant. The Island was no longer our home by this time; home was in Mozambique where we grew up, the place our hearts yearned for, but the chances of going back were gone forever.

There was still a lot of resentment against the Portuguese government among the refugees, as they called us. The feeling that we were abandoned to our fate by our own people was very clear in everyone's mind, and I don't think that our generation will ever forget that. Even if we have rebuilt a new life elsewhere, we will never feel at home. There was growing acceptance as time went on, but we could not forget what we had lost and left behind.

As a result of the resentment, the Portuguese community in Johannesburg celebrates the anniversary of the so-called "Revolution of the Red Carnations" in Portugal

As I Walk Through Life

on April 25, 1975. On that date, a group of people led a peaceful demonstration in Johannesburg, while at the same time a bomb destroyed the Portuguese consulate and everything in it. Several individuals were accused and arrested by the South African government, but since there was no proof, they were let go. After this incident people began to heal and move on with their lives; soon the war was nothing more than a memory. As God intended, time heals everything, and it was time to move on. After all, four years had gone by since the revolution.

The young man that I met just before going to Australia followed me to the refugee camp in Nelspruit, leaving his family behind. He also left the camp with us and stayed with my family. Two years later we got married, and three years later we moved to the United States, where his family had settled. His mother was born in the States and raised in Portugal, so during the revolution she reaffirmed her United States citizenship and brought some of the family with her. We had two sons and have been living in this country ever since, for the past thirty-three years. During this time I have had many good and not-so-good life experiences—but that is another story someday.

My siblings moved in different directions to different parts of the world, some with hardship and some with happy endings. My parents and two brothers have passed on and are resting in peace in Johannesburg next to one another. I remember the last time I asked Dad for his blessing; it was also the last time I saw him, and he had tears in his eyes as if he knew this was the last time we were to say good-bye. I had gone back home for Mom's funeral, so I held my dad at the airport for the last time to come back to America.

Lina DaPonte

As I Walk Through Life

One thing is for sure: the ones buried in Johannesburg will stay together forever. All the others, although separated by oceans, are in touch now and then. We do visit each other on occasion, especially the ones who can afford to travel, but life did not treat others so well, or else age is catching up, so the idea of crossing oceans is no longer appealing. Once in a while someone brings up the idea of a family reunion, but it does not seem to be possible.

I am sure that the memories we share of a lifetime growing up, the adventures, and even the hardships will remain with us throughout our lives and remind us never to give up or give in to what life brings. This is a legacy that I passed on to my sons, and I know that all my brothers and sisters are trying to do the same.

I don't regret any of the experiences that passed through my life. They made me who I am today. I look at the world through the eyes of that child, who grew up knowing that life is what you make of it at each particular moment. Yesterday cannot be changed—and it shouldn't: it happened for a reason. Tomorrow is full of possibilities, and even the painful moments can create beautiful memories.

When I reflect on past experiences, I miss Mozambique, because home is where the heart is. I like to remember the beautiful moments we had as a family, the love we had for each other, the laughter, and even the tears. We shed plenty, but even those tears left beautiful moments in our minds.

At night when I lie in bed, sometimes I can hear Mom and Dad calling us for that morning coffee that I have missed ever since. I can hear the ocean back in the Portuguese islands and the sound of the sea gulls. Then I let my mind travel to Africa, and I hear the laughs of the native children, the sound of the drums, even the canoes fighting the waves and the native fishermen humming a song that could only be heard in Africa. Then I go to sleep with a sense of peace and thankfulness for having had the opportunity to live a life that most people only read about.